I0484038

How to Master Online Customer Service

Copyright © 2015 by Lisa Harrison

First Printing: 2015

ISBN 978-1508422341

Lisa Harrison

POMO Creative

PO Box 4750

Sunshine Coast Mail Centre 4560

Australia

www.pomo.com.au

www.lisaharrison.com.au

Disclaimer:

Contents

Welcome

This book is the fifth in a series of books I am releasing in 2014-15; a complete guide to the world of social media for business.

The first book gave the fundamentals for setting up your digital footprint. The second focused on the art of building and maintaining networks and relationships as part of your online strategy. The third looked at e-marketing strategies, and the fourth covered how to use websites to your best advantage.

Having done everything necessary to create an attractive online presence, the next step is to ensure that once the customers arrive, they have the best possible experience; therefore ensuring that they return again and again (and tell all their friends about you, too).

This book is all about creating the systems and standards to make that happen. To make your business stand out not only for its slick website and fascinating Facebook page but also for the quality and helpfulness of the people behind the digital face.

I hope you enjoy reading it and working through the activities.

I wish you good luck in all your social media customer interactions.

Lisa Harrison

Introduction

"Your brand is only as strong as your last contact with your customer"

One of the most common hesitations that I see with clients looking to engage in social media is the realisation that conversations are happening all around and that they have no control.

This isn't a choice ("We should really let go of control") it's a fact and has been the case for a long time. But, until now they have been largely undocumented, un-indexed by search engines and not in any way facilitated by the company itself. The conversationalists were only as influential as their personal network allowed.

Now micro influencers have the power to reach millions of people around the world. Blogs and other social media outlets are indexed in search results right alongside company websites and portals.

The truth hurts, but it's not necessarily a bad thing.

Where social media shines brighter than any other marketing vehicle is **leveraging the truth to create stronger customer relationships** and **converting bad experiences into great ones**. Companies who don't listen to people in the first place have no place in social media.

There are only handful of businesses that see the value in customer input and take steps to make things better for them. They listen, when you call their 1800 number you talk to a person and, even if they don't solve your problem, you walk away with a positive feeling.

Supporting customer service is a perfect fit for social media, but it takes planning and strategy to make it pay off.

Have you heard the saying "your brand is only as strong as your last contact". By understanding these steps you will ensure that your online community will have a great experience all the time.

Getting the Most From This Book

This book contains all you need to know to design and put in place great customer service standards for your social media and digital activities. These facts and tips, plus advice and guidance will help you create standards that will transform your online business.

With the information in this book you will be able to:

- Provide a level of customer service to match the needs of your online customers.

- Develop organisational standards, policies and procedures for using social networks to provide customer service.

- Implement standards, policies and procedures to address customer service problems while using social networks.

- Provide administrative support within an organisation or support other individuals who have been delegated this responsibility.

- Implement and plan team building activities to ensure customers' needs and expectations are met.

Although this is not a coursebook, the emphasis is very much on helping you to use the knowledge and techniques to create real and tangible business benefits. With that in mind, the contents are based on:

- **Global best practice** – incorporating concepts from a range of customer service commentators and leading practitioners.

- **Practical application** – giving practical insights into developing and customer service standards that will genuinely lift the quality of your customers' experiences when dealing with your business online. Throughout this book, I encourage you to take action in a planned and strategic manner.

What Lies Ahead...

I've split this book into three chapters to give you a structure which will take you through the business of customer service in a clear and helpful fashion. To give you a road map for what you're about to read, here's a summary of those chapters:

Chapter 1: *Contribute to Quality Customer Service Standards*

Starting with first principles, customer service standards enable all employees to share an understanding of the organisation's expectations and the procedures they should follow to provide consistently high levels of service and how to meet customer needs.

Chapter 2: *Implement Customer Service Systems*

Having established clear and agreed standards, the next hurdle is to create a set of practical systems that enable your people to fulfil those standards. This is all about embedding high quality customer service systems into the way you use social media. What's more, you need to know how to identify problems and make the necessary adjustments to maintain (and improve) service quality.

Chapter 3: *Implement Team Customer Service Standards*

Finally, while individual customer interactions depend on individual employees, you also need to pay attention to how the team as a whole approaches customer service. This includes team building work to put everybody 'on the same page' and create a seamless and consistent experience for the customer no matter who they are dealing with.

CHAPTER 1
Contribute to Quality Customer Service Standards

Good (or even better, great) customer service is a strategy that all truly successful business owners understand and pay careful attention to because the one thing all successful businesses have in common is satisfied customers. And given that customer satisfaction comes from an experience that is not only good, but also consistent, what you need is a set of quality customer service standards.

Large or small, any business benefits from being able to access, interpret, apply and monitor customer service standards in the workplace. Such standards provide a framework which lets everybody know if they're 'doing it right' and provides you with a measurement system that lets you establish whether 'right' is 'good enough'.

Customer service comes first

Customer service can be defined as the range of education, support and care offered to existing and potential customers to ensure their needs are met. There's an old saying in commerce that says a happy customer might tell one or two people about their experience but an unhappy customer will tell 10. This number is much greater in the online world due to the easy nature of sharing information through social networks. Online, a seriously ticked-off customer might tell not just 10 people; they might also write a lengthy rant on their blog, post comments on their own or other people's social networking pages, write a negative review on a shopping website, or criticise you on forums and message boards. Maybe all of the above.

TIP: It's always about them (not you).

Unfortunately, once something has been written about you online it's very difficult to get it removed. This means that any prospective customer who decides to do a search on your business name could stumble across it. In other words, while good online customer service might cost a bit of time, effort and money, bad service could cost you dozens of prospective customers. Think how much losing even just 10 sales would cost you, and compare it to the extra sales you'll gain from making your customers happy.

What's really interesting is that many case studies show that building good customer service into a business increases a company's efficiency as well as its sales.

Customer service standards

In order to meet the needs of your customer base, a defined set of customer service standards will help ensure each individual is catered for. These standards will vary from company to company and industry to industry however the focus is always the same – positive consumer experiences.

High quality customer service standards need to specifically define:

- The organisation's customer service expectations.

- How the organisation interacts with customers during each stage of the buying cycle.

- The procedures employees should follow to provide consistently high levels of service.

- The behaviours employees are expected to demonstrate in order to provide a high standard of service.

It's very important employees in every part of the organisation understand the customer service standards and expectations. The organisation needs to document and disseminate standards so that all customers receive the same high level of care.

Nothing Less Than the Best

All customer-driven organisations have well-conceived and well-defined customer service standards. Customer-driven organisations are those that implement incentives for innovation, creativity and good customer service rewards in their plans and systems.

Customer-driven organisations include customer service and measures of customer service in their business plans and strategies; these, in turn, are then reflected in employees' job descriptions, in KRAs (Key Results Areas) and KPIs (Key Performance Indicators).

A truly customer-focused organisation refuses to accept less than the best and constantly creates and meets new standards of excellence. When the company culture is oriented on the customer, excellent customer service accepted as the norm.

Online Customer Service

E-commerce makes up a huge part of the Australian retail market and is growing with every economic quarter. More and more companies are capturing their target audiences online. To succeed, it's important to monitor your digital reputation as well as any comments, tweets or posts that mention your brand.

Consumers increasingly use social media to be more vocal than ever before about their purchasing experiences. Whether they have positive or – more importantly – negative experiences with a company, they tend to talk about them. It's critical for firms to make every effort to prevent the kind of poor online experience that leads to viral rants impacting on their brand.

TIP: We have seen sites such as Ebay and TripAdvisor incorporate customer feedback as part of the sales process, even sections asking for feedback on the helpfulness of information.

Social Media

In a traditional brick-and-mortar store, if a customer needs help he or she can look around and find someone with the answers. Online customers are learning that social media can be this source of contact. And just like in-store, if a customer is kept waiting too long they will look elsewhere. So do your best to respond with speed!

Social media offers your company so many opportunities to improve customer service standards. The goal with a brands' social media profile is to build a community of advocates. This will open dialogue around your company, your products and services and even your personnel. However, as already mentioned, if customers don't get a response they are satisfied with, they are likely to tell people about the bad experience they just received. What follows are some of the key online customer interaction points and strategies.

Live Chat

Live chat gives your customers a human contact point online. Live chat windows pop up on your website ensuring customers won't be directed away from your page to third-party sites. While it provides real-time help to more than one customer at a time, the downside is that you or your employees have to staff this chat utility. Make sure that your site clearly states when representatives are available to help. Once you have set your live chat hours, do your best to stick to them.

Order Tracking

Many of the inquiries that you'll receive from customers will be about the status of their orders. Automating the order-tracking process can free up time to manage the more pressing aspects of your business.

Many shopping cart programs offer integrated order tracking, and many items sent through the Australia Post delivery network have tracking capabilities, allowing you to view where the customer's item is during the delivery process.

(Of course, just because your customer receives the order does not mean that your work is done. Invariably, some percentage of merchandise will be damaged or even lost in shipping, or a customer may wish to exchange a product or have some other concern.)

Customer Support Ticketing

Implementing a support-ticket process can streamline your support process even further.

Support ticket applications are fairly simple: customers visit your site, click a support link, and are prompted to submit their order information. The support program will send you what the customer has submitted and you can craft your response. This system works very well if you have a lot of customers. However, if you have a small client base it may not be worth the time and energy to implement.

Phone support

If all else fails, there's always the telephone. It can be expensive and time-consuming to provide phone support, but sometimes it's the best way to communicate with your clients. You may be able to discuss and resolve in two or three minutes on the phone something that would take 10 emails.

> **TIP:** Even in the digital age it's not a case of 'internet killed the telephone conversation'. Customers will feel at ease if they converse with another human.

Customers also appreciate live phone support, and it can add a personal touch to your e-business. Most companies can't afford to provide 24-hour phone support, so don't forget to prominently post your phone hours. Reiterate these hours on your voice mail system or answering machine.

Automate Your Sales Process to Keep Customers in the Loop

Use auto responders to thank your customers for their order, welcome them to your opt-in email list, and send them order confirmations and other transactional emails, such as "your item has shipped" notices. Customers have come to expect these courtesies, but not everyone online bothers.

You can even add an element of surprise to these customer service emails by including a coupon for money off their next purchase or some extra information they'll find relevant to the product they've just bought. You may also want to ask if everything is all right with your customer's purchase or if there's anything further you can do.

This kind of follow-up can relieve possible feelings of buyer's remorse and reinforce positive feelings about your business.

It's important to keep these emails constantly updated. This takes time but if you don't keep on top of the auto responder information, you can turn consumers off. They will think twice before opening emails from your company if you've sent them outdated information before.

The FAQ page

A comprehensive FAQ page can answer most of the questions people might have about your products or services. You should also create an FAQ email address, such as info@mysite.com, and keep track of the fresh questions that customers or site visitors actually ask and then, having answered them, add the answers to your FAQ page.

With the common questions taken care of, you'll be freed up to spend time giving personal attention to the visitors who need it. The quicker you handle their concerns the more impressed they'll be.

Obviously, there will always be questions unanswered and answers that will not be specific enough. This is not a problem, as the main purpose of an FAQ page is to prevent the simpler, common questions from bothering the support team. Customers with a unique or complicated question (or a complaint) will have an alternative route to get their answer.

Taking the time to respond to customer concerns promptly and personally can generate a huge amount of goodwill for your business and referrals. Even angry customers can be turned into devoted fans if you pay attention to them, acknowledge your mistake (if you've made one) and fix their problem.

Make it Easy for People to Contact You

There will always be times when a customer needs to talk to or email someone directly, so don't hide your contact details away in a dark corner of your website, and always provide contact information on every message you send out.

Remember, personal contact does wonders for customer service so think about creating a customer service page on your site that includes the names, email addresses and phone numbers of people who can help with specific issues.

Many people with small e-businesses really don't want to talk to customers and actually make it hard for people to get in touch. But the worst thing you can do is look like you're hiding or just don't care.

Personalise and Segment Your eMail Messages

Use your customers' names in email subject lines and in your messages. according to Jupiter Research, only 4% of marketers personalise and segment their messages and yet personalised messages have almost twice the click-through rate of bulk email.

As an e-business owner, you can personalise and segment your communications with customers in many ways, including incorporating names and other pieces of information into emails, sending customers personalised birthday or anniversary greetings, or by providing tailored special offers.

Just be careful not to overwhelm customers with too much correspondence – find that healthy balance between informing and information overload.

Ask Your Customers How You Can Serve Them Better

It's been clearly shown that customer satisfaction is rated higher among people who have been asked what they want, even if their answers haven't been acted upon.

Yes, it takes time to put a survey together and collect the data. But simply asking what your customers want and how you can make your service better makes them feel listened to.

Customer support for online businesses isn't really that different from traditional business support. As long as you take care of your customers, they will keep coming back. Actually acting on their suggestions and improving your service is gold!

Develop and Refine Your Standards, Policies & Processes

Customer service standards might be set in a number of areas; for example, employee appearance, timing, communication, helpfulness, convenience and problem solving.

Useful and high quality customer service standards are:

- **Clear and unambiguous:** Employees must be able to understand the customer service standards. There should be no confusion as to what is expected of them.

- **Specific:** Standards that are too vague or general are of little value.

- **Concise, succinct and to the point:** Overly lengthy or complicated customer service standards can lead to misunderstandings. In addition to this, employees may ignore the standards because they are too complex and onerous.

- **Observable:** They can be easily identified in the workplace (e.g. are employees wearing uniforms?) and measurable (e.g. were customer phone calls answered within 3 rings?).

- **Realistic, practical and obtainable:** Customer service standards that are unrealistic will be disregarded by employees and cause them stress. Employees who are unhappy and overly stressed are unlikely to provide high customer service.

Effective and Ineffective Standards

In the following table, a number of high quality and low quality customer service standards for a restaurant have been listed to demonstrate the difference between effective and ineffective standards.

Low quality standards	High quality standards
Employees look neat and tidy.	Employees wear the uniforms specified in the dress code section of the employee handbook at all times.
Upon entering the restaurant, customers are greeted quickly.	Upon entering the restaurant, customers are greeted within 30 seconds.
Customers are seated as soon as possible.	Customers are seated within 3 minutes of entering the restaurant.
Customers' orders will be taken promptly.	Customers' orders will be taken within 5 minutes of being seated.
Employees will have a good knowledge of the menu.	Employees will know what ingredients are used in each menu item and are able to describe all meals in the menu as outlined in daily briefings by the chef.
Employees will think one step ahead of customers.	Customers will receive water refills without having to ask.
Meals will be made using fresh ingredients.	No frozen, out of date or stale ingredients will be used.

Bundling

In most instances, when customers make a purchase they have an expectation that the purchase will be accompanied by an associated level of care and acceptable quality and standards.

This is called bundling. You are not only providing a product to the customer, but also a service that must meet the customer's needs too. Customers expect bundles of products and services. When the newspaper is delivered in the morning, we are customers for both a product (the newspaper) and a service (delivery). When we purchase goods from a hardware shop we expect that the service offered in the store will enable us to make the correct purchase with ease. There will be numerous stores offering the same products, or range of products. It is likely that the customer's purchasing decisions will depend, to a large extent, on the service and standard offered as part of the bundle.

Of course there are other considerations that will affect the purchasing decision and which form part of the product/service bundle, including:

- Location

- Availability

- Timeliness

- Facilities

- Access

- Support-help desk or online

- Delivery

- Presentation

- Quantity

- After sales service

- Warranties/maintenance/repairs

All of these conditions become part of the bundle because they affect the consumer's choice. Customers look, either consciously or unconsciously, for something that distinguishes one product from another and adds to the perceived benefits of purchasing the product/service. It can be said that the customer is forming their own value proposition.

They are asking:

- Does this product meet my needs?

- Am I receiving a proper level of accompanying service?

- Am I happy with the overall product/service offering?

- Does this meet my perception (expectation) of value for money on the basis of the product, service or bundle?

If the total bundle does not meet the customer's needs, that is, poor service accompanies a good quality product, then the customer will most likely turn to your competitor (who provides both product and service at acceptable levels – even, in some cases, if the product costs a little more) for any further purchases.

Sellers are, therefore, able to distinguish their products from other similar offerings by varying the mix of product and service. Increasing the level of service accompanying the product sale can in itself provide the point of difference that ensures customers will purchase from you, not from your competitors.

Customers Using Social Media Expect a Very Quick Response

As shown by the response to this survey question: *"In general, how soon after you contact a brand, product or company on social media do you expect to receive a response?"*

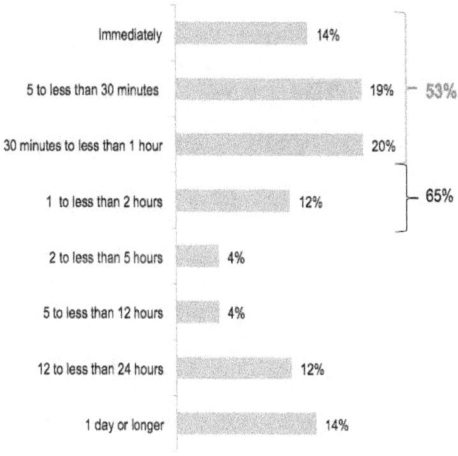

Source: Hubspot 2014. For more information on this head to http://blog.hubspot.com/marketing/twitter-response-time-data

Holding On to the Customer

The result of an unexpectedly high level of service is likely to be a willingness to become a loyal customer, ultimately transitioning to a brand advocate. These customers return because of previous experience; not because large amounts of money have been spent on expensive advertising, but because there is a worthwhile relationship. However, customer loyalty will only last as long as the actions of the organisation continue to earn the loyalty.

The next step is to then convert those loyal clients/customers to brand advocates. When a friend or associate is looking for a restaurant, or shipping line, or new shoes, customers tend to speak well of the organisation with whom they have satisfying relationships. This advertising is free and is, in fact, the best and most credible form of advertising.

Your attitude and that of the person in the organisation determines the extent of customer loyalty:

- treat each customer as an appreciated customer

- provide top quality as perceived by the customer

- build relationships

- create uniqueness

- under promise – over deliver

- work to retain your current customers

- have a positive attitude towards customers and towards work

- actively find out what your customers' needs are

- maintain high personal presentation standards

- develop a system for maintaining contact with loyal customers

- make customers who complain into loyal customers

- know your products and services and provide information about them

- communicate effectively and efficiently

- actively listen to what your customers are telling you

- ask questions in order to clarify customer needs

In addition to this, loyalty and repeat business both stem from:

- perceptions of a high quality product

- goods and services (bundles) which meet or exceed the buyer's expectations

- technology and technological development which meets the organisation's and customer's needs

- staff who are technically skilled

- organisational policies which support the recruitment and selection of customer oriented staff

- staff who have good interpersonal skills and make customers feel welcome, valued and important

- complaint systems which empower workers to efficiently and effectively manage and follow-up complaints and problems

- customer/client relationships that demonstrate commitment to the customer/client and to meeting their needs every time

- monitoring, measuring and continually evaluating success level.

> **TIP:** Why customers quit:
>
> - 1% die
>
> - 3% move away
>
> - 68% quit because of an attitude of indifference towards the customer by the staff.
>
> - 14% are dissatisfied with the product.
>
> - 9% leave because of competitive reasons.
>
> Source: How to win customers and keep them for life (2000) – Michael Leboeuf

The Evolution of Customer Service via Social Media

Customer service via social channels such as Facebook and Twitter, once considered an afterthought by most companies, has grown ever more important in recent years. As Conversocial Co-Founder and CEO Joshua March told AllFacebook, *"Over the past year, so many people woke up. Suddenly, every company we spoke with understood that social customer service was important."*

However, not every company is on board yet. March added, *"Most companies still view social just as a marketing channel,"* and went on to speak about the evolution of the social customer service sector over the past couple of years, telling AllFacebook:

How people communicate has been changing for the past couple of years. Facebook and Twitter are the communications channels for the next generation. Companies have spent billions of dollars educating their consumers to communicate with them through Facebook and Twitter. It's much, much cheaper to respond to people digitally on Facebook than to make a phone call.

Smart Use of Social Media for Customer Service

Brent Leary, co-founder and partner at CRM Essentials says those companies who adapt to offering customer service through social channels will have the chance to grow their customer relationships and make their products and services more appealing. Doing this, he says, isn't limited to large businesses:

> **TIP:** 80% of complaints received by an organisation are likely to have poor communication as their root cause, either with the customer or within the organisation itself.

"...because smaller companies are typically more agile and responsive – and providing social/mobile service is not cost prohibitive in many instances – this makes it possible for them to compete with larger companies who aren't able to quickly change processes and corporate cultures."

Four companies who are smart in the way they use social media to address customer service issues are Best Buy, Dell, JetBlue, and LL Bean.

EXAMPLE – ASOS
Fashion retailer ASOS created a dedicated Twitter channel solely for customer service. It's called "ASOS Here to Help."

Continuous Improvement

All business practices, including customer service and methods of addressing customer needs, must be subject to continuous improvement. This implies performance management, innovation and the continuous development of improvement ideas.

The old adage that 'It worked yesterday, therefore it should work today' no longer applies (if it ever did!) and in fact changes are occurring faster than ever before. Markets, customers and the whole world of business are in a constant state of change. In order to, at worst, keep up with and, at best, outstrip competitors – excellence in customer service is essential. No matter how good your product is, today's customer knows that they can purchase the equivalent from a competitor. In many cases, therefore, the service factor is the point of difference that determines whether customers will purchase from your organisation or look elsewhere.

What this means is that you and your organisation must constantly monitor your customers, their purchasing habits and any environmental (political, social, economic) trends that affect customer's value perceptions. Processes, procedures and customer service systems and standards must constantly be updated, changed and improved to ensure that your organisation maintains its competitive edge.

You must also:

- Know what the market wants now and is likely to want in the future.

- Know what your competitors are doing.

- Learn from your competitors.

- Learn from world's best practice ideas and strategies.

- Develop strategies to meet and exceed the expectations of your customers.

> **TIP:** A typical business only hears from about 4% of its dissatisfied customers. The other 96% just go away, and of those, 91% will never come back.
>
> Source: "Understanding Customers" by Ruby Newell-Legner

Edward Deming's PDCA

Quality improvement strategies are generally based on Edward Deming's PDCA (Plan, Do, Check, Act) cycle which is represented in the following diagram.

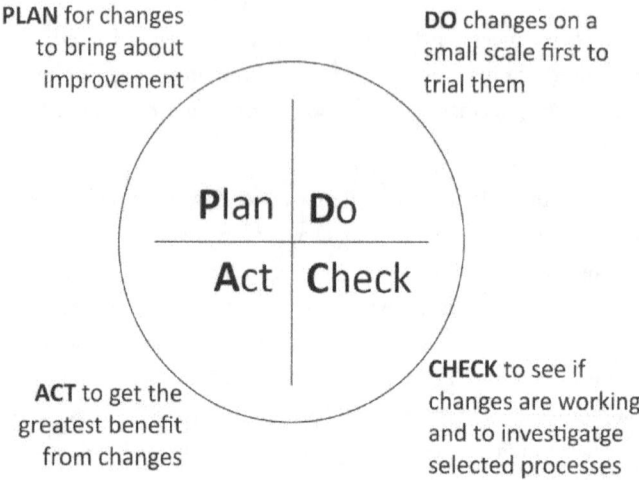

PLAN for changes to bring about improvement

DO changes on a small scale first to trial them

Plan | Do

Act | Check

ACT to get the greatest benefit from changes

CHECK to see if changes are working and to investigatge selected processes

The key to successful improvement strategies is gathering data and reviewing your organisation's performance based on solid evidence.

The Importance of Data

When implementing continuous improvement procedures the first questions to be asked are:

- What are our customers' and stakeholder satisfaction levels?

- Are we meeting and exceeding their expectations?

- What feedback do we get from our customers and how is this communicated to the employees within the organisation?

- Are all the employees in the organisation committed to quality and improvement?

- How can we improve our feedback systems and outcomes?

- Why might our customers leave and go elsewhere to purchase?

Continuous improvement involves the collection of data relevant to customer service and service strategies, analysis of the data and dissemination of the results. Results should be mapped against customer service KPIs, organisational expectations and actual levels of customer satisfaction, and then used to identify opportunities to enhance service and product quality.

Why Customer Service is SO Important

Even if you master each and every one of the internet marketing strategies out there – social media marketing, search engine optimisation, email marketing and the rest they're not worth a cent if you forget about customer service.

Over the last 5 years, the social network boom has created a new revolution in customer service. The reach and immediacy of Twitter, Facebook, and even Google+, has made the voice of the customer an extremely powerful force. Bad customer experiences can quickly snowball into online customer uprisings leading to PR disasters.

Online channels for customer service include:

- social media

- order tracking

- support ticketing

- phone support

- automating the sales process

- creating a FAQ section on your website

- making customer contact easy

- personalisation and inviting customer feedback

Remember, you need to have a clear (and data-based) understanding of what your customers' needs are. Package that with your products and services because bundling is a very powerful way to differentiate your brand from those of your competitors.

A high level of service is likely to lead to a willingness, on the part of customers, to become a loyal customer, ultimately transitioning to a brand advocate. What's more, the way to achieve that is through customer service standards that are clear and unambiguous, specific, concise and to the point, observable, measurable and realistic.

END OF CHAPTER ACTIVITY – Contribute to Quality Customer Service Standards

1. How do you provide good customer service as a part of the online sales experience?

2. It may be easier than you think to branch out; what alternative online channels could you use to support your customer service experience?

3. Think of a product or service which has been offered to you as a bundle. In your opinion did this bundle create loyalty with its customers? With you?

CHAPTER 2
Implement Online Customer Service Systems

Everybody, All the Time

Each and every person in the organisation must be committed to continuous improvement of online customer service systems, because success depends on input from every individual in the organisation – from senior executives through to the customer service representatives.

Organisations can encourage involvement by:

- Attacking processes, not employees – many quality problems occur because work systems are poorly designed; only a few problems are the result of employee error and often employee errors are system-related.

- Encouraging systems thinking; i.e. encouraging people who work in a system to make the effort to improve the system.

- Stripping down processes to find and eliminate problems that reduce quality.

- Instilling teamwork.

- Creating an atmosphere for innovation and permanent quality improvement.

- Reminding everyone that better quality pays.

- Developing consultative improvement plans.

- Encouraging employees to talk about their jobs and any associated problems.

- Encouraging employees to share any ideas they may have.

- Rewarding new ideas, innovation or improvement suggestions.

Organisations should discourage negative or non-productive thinking such as:

- I will deal with that later.

- Close enough is good enough.

- Who really cares?

- We cannot afford better quality.

- I do not have to deal with customers, so it is not up to me.

- It might work elsewhere but not in our industry.

- We must be doing Ok because we do not get many complaints.

Organisations can encourage positive thinking by:

- Encouraging online discussion through internal forums, supporting open and honest communication throughout the organisation.

- Developing effective teams.

- Leading by example.

- Involving people in decisions that affect them.

- Supporting effective relationship building.

- Encouraging personal and professional development of employees.

Customer Service is in the Hands of Frontline Staff

Good customer service does not just happen. Customer service has to be identified as an organisational goal, planned for, supported by resources, and it must be monitored and evaluated to ensure that organisations encourage all personnel to consistently provide high levels of customer service.

Consistency is the key to sustainable customer relationships. Customers expect the same levels of product/service each time they interact with a company. When they receive poor service or below expectation product they will look to your competitors.

There are a number of things that organisations can do to encourage employees to provide consistently excellent customer service. Organisations that look after their employees will find that they, in turn, will look after their customers.

Organisations that are concerned with maintaining high levels of customer service ensure that their staff are trained in both the technical aspects of their jobs, and in the ability to build relationships. They will also initiate incentive, recognition and reward systems for staff that demonstrate performance excellence.

The Importance of Written, Shared Standards

Assuming a company strives to build a positive business culture the following influential elements should be considered:

- Provide superior training to empower staff to do the right thing for customers with all of the tools needed to make their own decisions for the welfare of the organisation.

- Build the company's integrity by always following the Golden Rule and honouring return policies, special promotions, and treating both customers and other employees as if each person matters.

- Effective leadership guides the basis for a strong culture and the motivational tools needed to help employees understand the company's role as a positive business model.

- Instil a company focus on customers and fulfilling their needs and wants, Not just on the profit of each business transaction.

- Retain valuable employees by rewarding them with higher salaries, bonuses, rewards and recognition for jobs done well.

- Communicate with customers and display customer service phone numbers and email addresses on every page of your website(s) so customers know you're always willing to listen if there is a problem. Remember, most customers won't automatically tell a company what went wrong; they just leave and go on to the competition – you need to encourage that feedback.

- Don't make customers go through a maze of automatic questions when they are calling for customer service or make customers wait for any extended period of time.

- Hire the best employees and don't limit the time they should be on the phone or spending in person with a customer who needs help. Instead ask for public feedback and written communications from customers about their experiences. Grade employees on their service and what customers say about them – use rewards for the very best.

- Recognise employees to their peers which will then encourage other employees to excel.

Offer a Reward...

...for Employees

Giving staff verbal praise can have a significant impact on employees' motivation according to research compiled by employee engagement organisation, People Insight in 2012. The research looked into how cash-strapped businesses can motivate staff without the need for a pay rise, and was compiled from a range of employee engagement surveys. The findings were:

- 26% of employee respondents said managers do not identify training and development needs.

- 80% of employer respondents think their team is satisfied with their management skills, while only 58% of employee respondents agreed.

- 91% of employer respondents believe they spend time coaching their team, although only 40% of employee respondents agree.

> **TIP:** "You were hired because you met expectations, you will be promoted if you can exceed them."
>
> --Saji Ijiyemi

Such beliefs have the effect of seriously de-motivating staff. Praise and reward for good performance, however, motivate employees to improve their performance. Reward for performance helps to get maximum effort and performance out of employees, making reward a win-win situation for employees and employers. Reward systems also encourage other employees to emulate the behaviour of high performers.

...for customers

The phrase, "loyalty rewards" has something of a double meaning. Most people think of it as a marketing tool that encourages people to become repeat customers. This usually takes the form of punch cards for an eventual free cup of coffee at a cafe or a points system that leads to free or discounted food, hotel rooms, or whatever.

But another way to look at this is from the perspective of the brand: what are the benefits it reaps for inspiring the loyalty of its customers? And what does it take to inspire that loyalty? Rewards certainly help, but it's more important to focus on things like providing a great product or service, and being known for having top-notch customer service.

EXAMPLE - Zappos

Have you heard of Zappos? They're a US online retailer mega brand often referred to as a social media pioneer in marketing circles (for Twitter usage particularly). Yet, dig a little deeper and it becomes clear that a significant strategy is underpinning their success, and it's not all about social networks. It does, however, start to become obvious as

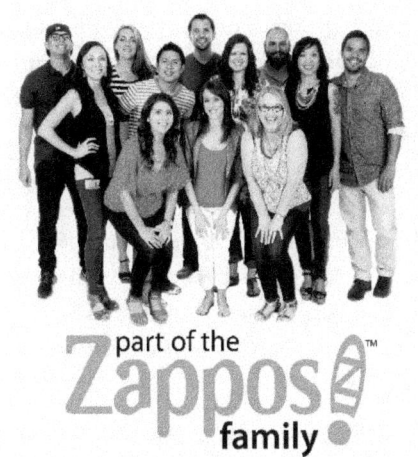

to why social media know-how is natural to them and necessary to help drive marketing.

Tony Hsieh, CEO of Zappos says simply,

"We pay more attention to our customers."

It's this simple, profound mentality that led to Amazon purchasing Zappos for a staggering $1.2bn in Nov 2009.

Tony goes on, *"People may not remember exactly what you did or what you said, but they will always remember how you made them feel."* This is the essence of how Zappos achieved their phenomenal success.

Apparently, it wasn't always this way and the Zappos brand evolution saw it go from simply having a strong customer focus to being passionate about how they make their customers feel.

One way in which Zappos engages with its employees is the Culture Book, which contains the unedited statements from staff, stating how they feel about working at Zappos.

5 things we can take from Zappos' success:

1. *Encourage customers to come back, and order more and often*

On any given day, about 75% of purchases from Zappos are from returning customers. Repeat customers order more than 2.5 times more in the following 12 months. Repeat customers spend more.

2. *Make it easy for customers to build your brand*

Superior experience drives word of mouth, so do the unexpected. Remove the risk of purchase and make it easy to return product for free. Fast, accurate fulfilment is worth talking about. Deliver "above and beyond" customer service. Drive people to the phone, be contactable and be open.

3. *Talk to people!*

Take the time to talk to people properly. *"The telephone is one of the best branding devices available."* At Zappos there are no call times and no sales-based performance goals for sales reps. Zappos will also pay you $2000 to quit, so only the best people who enjoy the job stay. The Culture Book makes it clear how Zappos do business and even underpins performance management.

4. *Build a culture that envelops customers and internal staff*

Zappos have "committable core values" that are clear, exciting and simple. It doesn't matter what your core values are as long as you commit to them and get internal alignment. Commit to a culture of transparency: "An Ask Anything Culture." Zapposinsights.com focuses on lifting the lid for customers and future employees

5. *Have a vision*

"Whatever you're thinking, think bigger," comments Tony. Does your company vision have real meaning? Without is there little chance of achieving any of the above. What would you be passionate about doing for 10 years even if you never made a dime? Tony concludes:

> If research tells Zappos that having vision, meaning and a higher purpose (as well as financial goals, we assume) leads to happiness internally and happy customers externally then what is your company's higher purpose? What is *your* higher purpose?

Now a social media power brand, $1.2bn later, and with publishers clamouring to tell his story, it's hard to argue with him really.

Rewarding the right way

Rewards based around customer service can contribute to employee enthusiasm and motivate employees to provide first-rate customer service all the time. However rewards systems must be structured so that they do not self-destruct. They must be structured in ways that encourage cooperation rather than competition.

Employees must support and assist each other, working together to achieve goals. High levels of in-house competition can create situations where information and knowledge are withdrawn in order to gain individual competitive advantage. Although programmes like inter-departmental competitions may seem advantageous in the short-term, they can have long-term repercussions that are decidedly unhealthy for the organisation individuals.

Rewards systems must be fair and equitable. If they are not they will have the opposite effect of that which is intended, leading to dissatisfaction, low morale and performance problems. An effective reward system ensures that each person receives appropriate recognition for the personal contribution they have made and the overall value of their position to the organisation, regardless of their level within the organisation.

The key is that rewards must be based on performance, not years of service, favouritism or anything else. Rewards systems will not work if employees have no confidence in them. If rewards are only given to managers, for instance, employees, who have contributed to their manager's success will become disenfranchised.

Reward systems should instead be based on clear criteria that are established before the system is introduced. Employees should understand exactly what performance or contribution constitutes rewardable behaviour or actions.

Rewards systems that are based on KPIs and efficiency targets will be the most relevant way to communicate the organisation's customer goals, as they are free from interpretation or manipulation.

Good reward systems

Offer both financial and non-financial rewards. Rewards for good performance could include:

- an increase in pay.

- financial bonuses.

- fringe benefits, e.g. the use of a company vehicle, payment of mobile phone bills, etc.

- gift vouchers, tickets to concerts, movies, sporting events and the like.

- taking an employee to lunch or dinner.

- holidays, extra leave.

- promotion, positive feedback, increased responsibility.

- work-life balance benefits such as flexible working hours or working from home.

- personal congratulations thanks from an employee's manager or the organisation's CEO or managing director.

- awarding shares in the company.

- trophies/ certificates.

- professional growth and development opportunities (e.g. educational programs, special training).

Whatever the reward and recognition system decided upon, it is important to ensure that the recognition:

- is sincere.

- is properly deserved.

- can be justified to other employees.

- does not get lost in the reward and the message of thanks.

- is recorded in the employee's human resource file.

Characteristics of a successful rewards systems will:

- be contingent on achieving desired performance levels rather than on merely doing certain tasks.

- be meaningful and valuable to the individual (i.e. the reward may be perceived to be valuable to the individual, what may be coveted by one individual may not be valued by another).

- match reward to achievement.

- be timely; rewards should be awarded as soon as possible after the behaviour that merited the reward, the sooner the reward the greater the impact and the stronger the perceived link between performance and rewards).

- be based on objective and obtainable goals.

- be open to everyone (i.e. everyone can win).

- be specific so the person knows why they are getting the reward (describe what the employee did to help the organisation).

- reward employees publicly; when employee's work is openly rewarded, they feel more valued and appreciated and other employees are encouraged to work towards the attainment of rewards.

Training Employees

Knowledge of good customer service procedures is not innate. Employees need to be trained to provide good customer service consistently. An effective induction and training programme, matched to appropriate performance appraisals will benefit the organisation, the customer service employees and, ultimately, the customers.

People will do their jobs competently when they have been given the knowledge, and the skills (competencies) that will enable them to perform to the required standards.

These days, social media has transitioned from 'hype' to 'opportunity'. The key is ensuring employees understand how to use social media for business.

Educating and training employees about the opportunities and risks of social media is the best approach to mitigating the challenges presented by this new media. By creating policies and guiding principles for social media use in the business environment, as well as providing sufficient training, companies can familiarise employees with the unique characteristics and potential risks of social media.

Companies should effectively encourage the adoption and use of social media for business benefit, while ensuring the risks are properly managed. A good training programme, that includes interactive scenarios and assessment questions, provides a 'failsafe' environment where employees could test their knowledge of social media and familiarise themselves with appropriate business use. Also, training programmes are a good way to address questions about the delineation between private and business use of social media.

Use Customer Feedback in Employee Training

We all need feedback on what we are doing. Plays and films are reviewed by critics. *Choice Magazine* reports on the quality, durability and value for money of numerous products and services. Many consumers make decisions based on this information. Similarly, organisations need feedback on how customers perceive the service they are receiving.

The only true judge of whether your organisation is succeeding is the customer and as such, an your customers are one of the most valuable sources of information you have. Feedback and input from customers should be a constant part of the organisational planning, monitoring and evaluation processes. Data collected from customers, both internal and external, enable you to measure levels of success and to make changes and improvements to products and services as required.

Customer feedback is absolutely vital for the measurement of organisational success. Unfortunately, however, in some organisations gathering feedback is seen as an insignificant priority, when compared to making sales and relating directly with customers: a very short-sighted and non-productive attitude. The purpose of collecting customer feedback is to enable organisations to understand customer expectations as fully as possible in order to meet or exceed them.

Being busy is not necessarily a measure of success. Many businesses and the people they employ may appear to be increasingly busy, but in effect the business may be declining. This could happen if the market was rapidly expanding. Although your sales and customer numbers are increasing, they are not increasing in proportion to the total market. In other words, the organisation is actually losing market share. Failure to analyse and use customer information will lead to unrealistic acceptance of increased sales figures as a measure of success.

Organisations that do not collect, measure and analyse customer feedback will:

- not know what your customers' needs and expectations are.

- have no idea of the levels of customer satisfaction.

- not know what your customers truly think of them.

- not know the degree to which they are actually meeting customer needs and expectations.

A Culture of Customer Service

In the best performing companies, CEOs ensure that employees at all levels understand their customers and are given the tools to serve them well.

Leadership must communicate the importance of customer service and ensure that all employees, even those without direct customer-facing jobs, understand how their work serves the customers.

Management must regularly interact with customers so they understand evolving customer needs.

Most importantly, frontline customer service workers must be empowered to actually solve problems on the spot.

Provide Consistent Service Across All Channels

Continuously collect comprehensive customer feedback across the whole customer experience—not just via each channel.

As communication preferences change, we need to adapt our services to interact with our customers, when and how they prefer.

Consistency of service across channels is critical – a customer who gets an answer on the phone should receive the same answer in-person at a local office, via the website, over email, or via a mobile device.

Gathering Customer Feedback

Historically, customers have either filled in a survey on the website, or placed a call into the contact centre when they want to provide "feedback." Organisations would use this as a way of gauging the sentiment of their customer base. The problem with this approach is you are hearing only from customers who decide to give you feedback. What about all your other customers or prospects who decide not to get in touch? What was their feeling about the experience they had with your company?

The reality is, to obtain the true "voice of the customer," we need to gather direct feedback, but we should also be making use of all the other sources of information available to us.

Social media has obviously provided a high profile channel for customers to provide indirect feedback to organisations, but a lot of other sources exist within the contact centre to help companies gather a more complete picture.

Why Collect Customer Feedback?

Customer feedback provides the information necessary for:

- identifying problems and generating problem solutions.
- identifying what is working.
- accessing individual and organisational performance.
- initiating quality control measures.
- managing operations.

- developing continuous improvement activities.

- designing and developing reward and recognition systems for employees.

- developing and planning new goals.

- managing finances and capital effectively.

- exploiting current successes and taking advantage of new opportunities.

- determining the future buying needs of current and potential customers.

- improving their customer service standards before customers defect.

The Importance of Online Customer Reviews

Reviews are an essential ingredient your website needs today, especially if you want to stay ahead of the pack. Social commerce company, digitalvisitor.com found positive reviews online are almost as influential as price when it comes down to making decisions to booking travel options online.

A recent online travel booking poll, conducted by Webcredible, revealed 29% of consumers considered positive reviews as the most likely factor to make them book a holiday online. The only factor identified as more important than reviews was price, at 38%.

A review that may seem negative to one person can be positive in another person's view. Take for example a review of a hotel that describes it as 'not child friendly'. A couple looking for a romantic weekend getaway would not see this as a deterrent for booking, and would most likely welcome this fact.

> **TIP:** A negative review is not always bad for sales.

Organisations that really want to make the most of their customer reviews now and in the future, will be those that consider how to make them relevant for each online visitor. The more relevant and appropriate the reviews included on your website are to the potential customer, the greater the influence is on the buying process.

Plus, research has proven the importance for organisations to be wary of censoring the negative reviews as 70% of people trust reviews more when they can see bad reviews as well as good. Furthermore, 38% of shoppers are more likely to read the bad reviews than the good ones but 95% of people said they will still buy a product with a bad review.

Make the Most of Reviews on Your Website

Make it as easy as possible for your visitors to add reviews with convenient avenues for uploading of their comments, photos and videos.

Display your reviews in the correct place, such as:

- a selection below the fold on the homepage.

- a selection on secondary landing pages.

- specific reviews on product/service information pages.

Ask your customers to leave a review in your marketing and promotional material. For example, you may want to include a link on your receipts, or on any email communications that go to your customers.

Incentivise: give your customers a reason to review your organisation or service. For example, you might want to offer them the opportunity to enter a competition, or provide a coupon or discount off their next purchase if they leave a review.

If you have received a compliment from a customer, be it via email or verbally, take this opportunity to tell them that you appreciate reviews, and give them the website address where they can post a review to spread the good word.

If you discover positive comments about your brand, products or services on any other social networking sites, contact the user with a link to where they can add a review on your website.

Work out which department or who in your organisation is responsible for responding to the comments and ensure that each and every review (whether positive or negative) is responded to in a professional and timely manner.

Holistic Customer Feedback

To gauge the true "voice of the customer" multiple channels, like market research groups and web interactions data, need to be employed. Some ways of getting feedback from customers include:

Informal Assessments – Customer Communication

Employees can gather customer feedback simply by talking to their customers and make casual inquiries about product/service quality. It's often through informal discussions that organisational personnel become more aware of the needs and expectations of their customers.

Surveys and Questionnaires

Surveys are often used to gauge client satisfaction with customer service or quality.

Many organisations use online surveys, which allow people to answer questions online. This practice increases the likelihood that respondents will complete and return surveys, as it is much less time-consuming and much more convenient.

Interviews

Interviews can be an effective way to ensure that questions are put directly to the respondents and that discussions about the issues in question can be held. Information can be gathered from interviews that may be difficult to collect through surveys and questionnaires because the interviewer can ensure that the respondent understands questions and clarification is easy if the respondent can ask questions.

Interviews can be carried out on the telephone, in which case, many of the questions used are designed to elicit short answers (e.g. using yes/no questions or questions that provide limited responses, pick one of, say, three alternatives).

Face-to-face, one-on-one interviews are quite common as are group interviews in which a facilitator may put questions to the group.

Focus Groups

A focus group is an interview conducted by a facilitator in a non-structured manner with a small group of respondents. The facilitator leads the discussion, encouraging group members to talk openly, with the purpose of gaining personal insights from the members of the group, from a particular target group who have common interest in the issues to be covered. One of the greatest benefits of a focus group is that there can be unexpected data revealed from the free-flowing group discussion and the facilitator can also pursue a more detailed examination of the issues raised by asking questions in the open forum.

Feedback Forms

Feedback can also be gathered on generic feedback forms. These can be used to collect suggestions for improvement, compliments, complaints, questions and comments. These forms allow customers to provide organisations with the feedback they want to provide and not just answer questions posed by the organisation, as is often the case when customers are asked to complete surveys. Feedback forms are often available on an organisation's website.

Day-to-Day Feedback

Customers are continually providing information as to what they want and do not want, or their satisfaction and dissatisfaction, but often the feedback does not reach the people in the organisation who are in a position to do something to improve the situation.

The answer to the problem is to open up the channels of communication, recognise that people of all levels, if encouraged, can and want to contribute to the organisation's success. If people feel that their contribution is not going to be listened to or not warranted, important information for the organisation's success will not be forthcoming.

Always Keep the Channels of Communication Open

Many organisations want more occasional feedback from their customers. They want a relationship. Some businesses attempt to create inducements for customers to become regular users of the goods and services offered. Airlines use frequent flyer schemes, or they use reward card systems like FlyBuys.

Whatever the scheme, it's useful if you have a large mailing list which can be used to send out well-targeted information to customers. You can use the established relationship to obtain feedback. Success can be measured in the way in which you are able to keep channels of communication open and handle customer feedback in a positive, sensitive and polite manner.

Other data and feedback gathering methods include:

- direct contact with face-face questioning

- mystery shoppers

- product testing – to provide feedback on quality and variation

- market research

Using Feedback Data

Gathering information and then not acting upon it is a waste of time and resources. It is in fact, counter-productive, in that customers who have taken the time to respond to your request for information will take their custom elsewhere as soon as they realise that there is no response to their concerns. You should plan to act on the data they provide and use it to improve operations. Analysis of the data might show, for instance, that a number of customers are complaining about the same issues. In such cases it will be necessary to make changes to operations so that customer needs and expectations can be met.

Identifying areas in need of improvement could be discussed at team meetings or a formal proposal might need to be submitted to management. Team or division meetings also give the customer service staff opportunity to discuss issues or complications they have encountered and get input from other team or group members.

The data you collect and which is analysed should be used to:

- find areas of current excellence.

- find problems.

- improve opportunities.

- implement new revenue raising activities.

Improve the online experience

The overwhelming majority of today's websites suffer from four types of common design flaws that arise from failing to account for the customer experience. These problems hurt the business by making it hard for customers to achieve goals like buying products, opening an account, or using self-service features.

1. *Details* – Users have specific goals when visiting a site, like finding information to make a purchase. Companies need to strike at the heart of what their customers need/want to know and are looking for. For example, a business traveller who wants to find a hotel with a well-equipped gym needs the site content to tell her if a gym exists and what equipment she'll find in it. If she doesn't find that content, she'll either phone the property – running up the company's service costs – or book a room with a competitor that has better information.

2. *Navigation* – Having fantastic tools and rich content means nothing without well-designed navigation that creates awareness of what the site has to offer and streamlines the paths to user goals. Visitors abandon sites when forced down cumbersome paths or get lost with company-centric menu categories. Companies that change menu structures to match the way users think, improve metrics like number of product views, total orders, and conversion rates.

3. *Presentation* – Well-designed web pages help companies draw visitors' eyes to essential content and function while minimising distractions. Improve the visibility and location of links to top categories.

4. *Trust* – For customers to enter in their personal information or credit card details requires that they trust the site to handle it properly. Broken links, lack of availability, and slow download speeds significantly undermine consumers' perception of a site's credibility. Furthermore, hidden privacy and security policies erode that trust. The simple practice of surfacing privacy and security policies costs virtually nothing and greatly improves the customer experience, which makes it one of the most highly leveraged design fixes.

Identifying the problems and solutions

The best thing to do is to think like the first-time buyers visiting your website. Your business is an unknown commodity to these people, and they have many unanswered questions: Is this a legitimate company? What if I pay for a product, and they don't ship it? Who do I contact with a question or complaint? How do they handle returns and refunds? Customers who have already bought from you had these questions answered when they placed their first orders.

> **TIP:** The goal of any commercial website should be to make customers feel like they're actually holding or seeing your product in person.

One way to increase customer comfort levels is to have information-driven pictures accompanying your product descriptions so there's no confusion about the products. It's also important to make your site easy to navigate so it quickly answers customers' questions about deliveries, payments, shipping and refunds. And make sure your website contains your company's complete contact information, including the company's mailing address, phone numbers and important email addresses.

The Value of Complaints

Possibly the most important feedback customers can give you comes in the form of complaints. Complaints tell you what customer service problems exist and allow you to make adjustments to ensure continued service quality. The role of a complaint management system is of immense importance. It can form the basis for the deepest improvement initiatives.

It is, therefore, essential to develop a culture in which complaints are welcomed and are addressed properly. Your organisation should have complaint management systems in place, with information about the system disseminated to customers.

Make it possible for customers to complain. Make it comfortable for customers to complain. Let them know that you welcome their complaints, ideas and suggestions. Make the customer aware that you are concerned about their welfare, that you value their input and that you will follow-up on complaints and suggestions.

When a customer registers a complaint it is important that you listen carefully and actively, empathise, are polite and friendly, ask appropriate questions and negotiate a satisfactory resolution. By asking questions you will be able to determine the true nature of the complaint and assure the customer that you are concerned with resolving the issues.

Ask open-ended questions to elicit more information, allow the customer to speak freely without being interrupted and paraphrase the complaint to ensure that you are both in agreement on the nature of the complaint. Remain calm, always speak politely and assure the customer that you will do everything you can to assist them. Never raise your voice, abuse the customer, denigrate their complaint, use sarcasm or make the customer feel that they are unimportant.

All organisations should be aware of the need to consistently provide excellent product quality and service. To do this you need to encourage your customers to complain and to take visible action to resolve complaints. You should thank the customers who complain for their contribution to your success.

Why Do So Many People Not Bother to Complain?

Because they:

- Do not want to make a scene.

- Do not want retribution for a complaint i.e. a staff member 'spitting' in their drink or meal.

- Do not have the time or energy.

- Are convinced that the store or outlet is not interested and will not respond well.

When customers overcome their reluctance and make a complaint, they should leave feeling gratified that you took the time to listen and to find a solution (or at least a compromise), believing that you offer good customer service, your product/service guarantees are genuine, and that you personally care about your customers. A properly handled customer complaint can transform a complaining customer into a loyal, long-term customer who will tell friends and acquaintances about the good service they received.

Complaint Tracking

Having determined what the complaint is, you will need to record the appropriate information in your system. Your enterprise will have specific policies and procedures for you to follow when a customer chooses to register a complaint.

When recording complaints for your register you need to ensure:

- Data is as per your organisation's policies and procedures.

- The nature of the problem is clearly stated.

- Any background to the problem is clearly described.

- The details of the problem are specific, clear and true.

- Data is in a form that can be analysed.

- That you and the customer agree on the nature of the complaint and that the summary of the information you are recording is acceptable to the customer.

Analysis of customer feedback in the form of complaints or problems can show up trends or particular areas of concern. For example, your record might show that one particular product is returned by, or causes concern to, a large number of customers. You would, therefore, investigate further to determine the real cause of the problem. As a result, the manufacturing process might need to be re-designed, quality monitoring methods might require changes or the product might be withdrawn and replaced by a higher quality product. Thus the information gathered from a number of customer complaints contributes to the organisation's continuous improvement processes.

An organisation's complaints management system should have the following characteristics and elements:

- Commitment to seeking efficient and fair resolution of complaints at all levels of the organisation.

- Fairness, equity and recognition of the right of both the complainant and the organisation.

- Resources to deal with the volume of complaints – technological and personal.

- Delegated authority to handle complaints.

- System visibility so that both employees and external customers are aware of the system.

- A guarantee that complaints are dealt with speedily and complainants are treated courteously.

- Remedy applications so that issues are resolved and managed appropriately.

- Improvement processes to address systemic and recurring problems.

- Follow-up procedures to check problem resolutions.

- Accountability and documented performance standards against which performance is regularly reported.

- Review and feedback loops so that the complaints handling system is itself regularly viewed.

Resolving Complaints

There are a number of steps that should be followed when endeavouring to resolve complaints.

Step 1 involves identifying and defining the problem. Start with a definition of the desired situation which is compared to the current or actual situation.

Step 2 requires an analysis of the gap between current and desired situation. At this stage you should identify the reason/causes of the problem.

Step 3 is all about gathering data which can be analysed to give reliable, relevant, valid and timely information related to the problem and possible solutions. Any decision based on invalid, incorrect or unreliable data is an unsound decision.

Step 4 is solution generation. In order to make the most effective decision, generate as many alternative solutions as possible. Involve others in the analysis, particularly those likely to be affected by either the problem or the change. The input of others may increase the number of alternatives offered, thus improving the quality of the solution. Also those staff who have been involved in resolving an issue are more likely to be committed to implementing the solution. (See the next section for more detail).

Step 5 is analysing all the alternatives and making a choice. Which alternative or combination of alternatives will best suit the organisation's and customer's needs, thus improving the organisation's customer service standards.

Step 6 is about implementing the chosen solution.

Step 7 involves monitoring and evaluating the solution/new processes. Your intention is to ensure that desired and actual solutions are one and the same; that the solution is, in fact, closing the identified gap between desired and the actual situation.

Finding a Solution

When it comes to Step 4 in the complaint resolution process, there are a number of tools that can be used to generate solutions, including:

Brainstorming

This involves bringing together a group of people who meet to generate ideas and alternatives for problem solving. Ideas, no matter how odd or far-fetched, are proposed and recorded, regardless of viability, relevance or possible success, individuals are encouraged to think unusual thoughts and to be creative and innovative.

The Nominal Group Method

Similar to brainstorming, group members must be physically present; however, they are required to generate their own ideas independently, without any group interaction. Before any discussion takes place, each member of the group writes down their ideas.

The Delphi Technique

This technique involves a group of people sharing ideas without needing to be physically present. A carefully designed questionnaire, intended to elicit responses concerning the problem at hand, is distributed. Respondents generate various solutions.

Quality Circles

This involves groups of people meeting regularly to discuss issues or problems that have occurred in the past month, week, etc. and then generating innovative solutions to those identified problems. These groups can work well when there is a high level of employee involvement and the focus is on quality and productivity improvements.

The Scenario Technique

This technique was developed in the United States by the Rand Corporation. Multiple scenarios, originating from the same starting point, can be created, with variables added or considered. Scenario writers often tend to present a best case and worst case scenario with several intermediary alternatives.

When making a choice about solutions you need to ask:

- Does the proposed solution meet the essential criteria?

- Is it a desirable option?

- Will personnel in the workplace be able to cope with the proposed change?

- What adaptations will others need to make, and is this reasonable?

- Will others support the decision?

- Are the resources available to support the choice?

- Can you justify your choice?

- Will it work?

Post-Complaint Communication

Once you have decided upon the adjustments that need to be made to service delivery, all employees who will be affected by the change need to be advised. For this, it helps to have a standard communication plan.

In developing a template communication plan, the following questions need to be asked and answered:

- Who needs the information, why and when?

- What information do they need?

- What does management want to say?

- What medium should be used to communicate the information?

The communication plan should inform employees about:

- The aims/objectives of service delivery changes or adjustments.

- How these changes are linked to organisational or business goals.

- The reasons behind the changes.

- The implications of any changes.

- Any expected benefits of service delivery changes.

- How existing policies and procedures will be affected by service delivery changes.

- How employee roles, work, actions or performances will be affected by service delivery changes.

- What employees need to do; i.e. what is required of them.

- Who they should contact for further information or if they have any queries or concerns.

- The timeline for implementation of service delivery changes/adjustments.

Effective communication is needed in order to gain the trust and commitment of employees in service delivery changes and adjustments. More than one communication channel will need to be used to ensure that all employees receive the important information about any service delivery changes and adjustments.

Methods of conveying information to employees might include:

- Through the organisation's intranet

- Special presentations (including video)

- Team meetings

- Emails or newsletters

- Fact sheets

- Notice boards

- Training sessions

Whilst face-to-face meetings are a valid communication channel, it's important for organisations to support this with written forms of communication also. Thus making sure all employees have received the relevant information and have access to it later for reference.

All written communications should be in plain English and easily understood by all employees and translated for speakers of non-English-speaking backgrounds.

Special consideration might also need to be applied where there are employees with disabilities such as sight impairment or learning disabilities.

Finally employees need to feel that they are able to approach managers with any queries that they may have. Communication needs to be a two-way process and a positive communication climate is desirable.

Amplify the Power of Your Customer Advocates

The flip side to the complaining customer is the customer advocate (and if a complaint dealt with professionally and well, you can turn one into the other). An online method of encouraging customer advocacy is the social referral programme.

Social referral is an end-to-end marketing programme that enables brands to reach out to highly-engaged, loyal customers and turn them into "social advocates" – who, in turn, refer the brands and products or services they sell to their friends and social communities. If your brand can properly harness the power of a social referral programme, you can tap into a new, high-value marketing channel.

Here are the top 5 tips for amplifying the power of your customer advocates:

1. **Make referring easy**

   Make it easy for customers to share your brand's products and/or services with their friends. Include relevant sharing options (email, Facebook, Twitter, Google+, etc.). PURLs, or personal URLs, are also a great sharing option, as they can be shared across any channel – blogs, instant messages and social networks.

2. **Promote across channels**

   Driving awareness of the social referral program is critical to its success. Brands should leverage their owned assets, including corporate websites, email lists, as well as social networks – Facebook, Twitter, Google+, LinkedIn, etc. – to promote the referral program to their customers and drive the highest participation rate.

3. **Increase participation with incentives**

   Give your customer advocates a compelling reason to share with their friends. This could be an internal offer (free goods, discounts, or loyalty points), gift cards, or charitable donations. Make sure there is an incentive for their friends to make sharing more attractive and improve the probability of converting friends into new customers.

4.   Make it personal

Providing a simple, personalised experience for referred friends ensures the highest level of trust, engagement, and participation in a social referral program. Ensure that friend messages and landing pages are personalised, concise, and have a clear call to action to drive optimal results.

5.   Add recognition and gamification

Tap into human behaviour and the desire to compete, excel, and be recognised for achievement. Add in leader boards and scoring to your referral program to foster participation and additional sharing.

Brands have an enormous opportunity to foster their customer advocates to create an incredibly powerful marketing channel via social referral programs. Done correctly, social referral programs can amplify a brand's reach exponentially.

Coordinating Quality & Delivery to Meet Standards

Some of the factors affecting business success include product and service quality. Quality means doing the right thing at the right time, over time. That is, customers expect that the quality of an organisation's service and products will meet their expectations each time they have contact with the company.

Organisations and their employees should strive to meet quality standards 100% of the time. There are serious repercussions of giving less than 100%.

Know your market

Variations in product quality and service must be minimised so that they meet customer expectations every time. Customers today are more discerning, more aware and better educated than before. They know their rights and understand the range of choices open to them. They will no longer unthinkingly accept whatever goods and services the manufacturers choose to manufacture or suppliers choose to supply.

Badly-made products are quickly rejected. This results in lost revenue plus the cost of designing the product and the operations to produce it, coupled with the costs of marketing processes, manufacturers determining the standards and style of products required by their target market. It is therefore imperative prior to initiating the manufacturing and marketing processes, manufacturers determine the standards and style of product required by their target market.

Poor quality products harm a company's good name and reputation. Add to this the staggering rate of consumer defections from any company, even when things are going well and the cost can be enormous. The combined cost of product failures and customer defections represents billions of dollars in lost revenue and profit.

It is not only products that need to meet quality standards but also services and customer service. When customers purchase goods they are purchasing the bundle – the product plus the associated services – as discussed in Chapter 1.

Their perception of quality will be influenced by how welcome they feel when entering into a transaction, the degree of friendliness, assistance and relationship building that the service person puts into the transaction. The direct contact between the customer and organisation or organisational representation will determine whether customers purchase from your organisation and/or have a continuing purchasing relationship with you and your organisation.

It is, therefore, in your own interest to provide both a quality product and a high level of customer service.

Every Employee Should Know Why Customer Service is Important

Staff need to see the links between their jobs, the organisation's income, personal income and customer satisfaction.

Ultimately, customer service staff need to understand that it is the customer who pays their wages. There is a direct link between their job and an organisation's customers.

Where quality service standards are delivered consistently:

- Employees will communicate with customers in a manner which promotes goodwill, trust and satisfaction, ensuring needs and requests are met.

- Employees will uncover customer needs and satisfy them by identifying the products, explaining possibilities, service and facilities their organisation offers.

- Employees will provide friendly and courteous offers of assistance beyond the customer's original request.

- Employees will promote the organisation's service and products to encourage repeat visitation.

- Telephones will be answered promptly.

- Customers will be given valuable and reliable information.

- Invoices and bills will be prepared accurately and on time.

- Promotion and advertising will not mislead customers.

Quality Control

This can be managed through simple inspection processes. Where product/service standards are set, the product or service is examined to assess the degree of conformity. Output that is acceptable is distinguished from poor quality output. Below standard or unacceptable outputs will be scrapped or revoked.

The purpose of a quality assurance system is to assure the customer that the organisation's products or service are meeting the purpose for which they are intended and will consistently meet customer expectations. To be able to give this assurance, an organisation's quality system must be in line with agreed standards. There are both International standards and Australian standards for quality systems.

Australian Quality Assurance Standards require specific procedures for an organisation's operations documentation. This documentation process can be broken into three-parts:

1. A quality manual identifies the organisation's policy and quality objectives, outlining the controls that are in place in all operations areas, i.e. management, purchasing, training, occupational health and safety, etc.

2. A procedures manual identifies responsibility, authority, processes and procedures – the who, what, when, where, how and why of the organisation's operations.

3. Detailed work instruction manuals to inform personnel of roles, responsibilities and methods of work so that they are clearly understood.

Expectations of Suppliers and The Supply Chain

Your business is part of what can be called a supplier-customer chain. Depending on where you are in the chain, the end–users of the product or service are not always direct customers of the manufacturer/producer.

Products and services move through the chain in a series of inter-connected events. At every stage of the customer-supplier chain, at every interface, customer expectations and the building of good customer relationships are of paramount importance. A break in the supplier chain means not producing the product/service to meet a customer's needs and will inevitably lead to the customer purchasing elsewhere.

When everyone in the production chain passes products and services that are of the same high quality they expect from the suppliers, the end product will also be of high quality.

Why Online Customer Service Systems are Vital to Business

Good customer service does not just happen. Customer service has to be identified as an organisational goal, planned for, supported by resources and it must be monitored and evaluated. To recap, customers today are more discerning, more aware and better educated than before; they know their rights and understand the range of choices open to them.

Staff and customer reward systems are an essential component but they must be structured so that they do not self-destruct. They should encourage cooperation rather than competition.

Effective communication is needed, not only to gain the trust and commitment of employees in service delivery changes and adjustments but also to build and maintain customer trust. Customers need encouragement to give you feedback. In most cases, people choose not to complain because they have no faith in the ability of the person to whom they are complaining to actually resolve issues or because they believe that their complaint will be met with either inaction or with indifference.

Once received, feedback should be can be acted upon as quickly as possible, if not immediately. Effective and efficient information-sharing at all levels with the organisation is essential to fostering a customer focused workplace culture. An efficient flow of information and greater opportunities for employees to perform to the expected standards equals greater levels of customer satisfaction.

Each and every worker should understand the operations of their organisation and the link between their job and their customer or end-user. Ultimately, customer service staff need to understand that it is the customer who pays their wages. There is a direct link between their job and an organisation's customers.

END OF CHAPTER ACTIVITY – Implement Online Customer Service Systems

1. Research your company, or one you are familiar with, and describe how they communicate changes to customer service standards within the organisation.

2. How could this process be improved?

CHAPTER 3
Implement Team Customer Standards

No matter how automated your website is, it's inevitable that some interactions will require some direct customer contact; often via a contact centre or other team of customer service employees. However, most customer contact centre staff have no idea what the caller saw or did online or where things might have gone wrong. This lack of visibility creates a multi-channel customer experience gap that results in slower problem resolution, lower first-call resolution rates, lower customer conversion rates and ultimately less satisfied customers. To close this gap, customer service teams need visibility into the online experience of each customer.

Create a Great Customer Service Team

Teams need to be well-structured to increase the team's ability to deal with a variety of tasks with minimum pressure. In an ideal world, a customer service team should consist of people with different backgrounds and experience. Diverse teams can take longer to bind, but ultimately have a much richer and wider pool of experience to draw upon. This allows staff to work to their strengths and interests, making them happier and more fulfilled. By contrast, teams of similar people can be quite uncreative in the way they approach problems, reducing effectiveness.

Structuring work around teams (rather than the other way around) is seen as the way to increase productivity and improve both quality standards and customer service. It reduces the formal divisions between jobs and enables better levels of training, coaching, mentoring and multi-skilling staff.

The Effective Team

The characteristics of an effective team are:

- Openness and honesty.

- Coordination, support, trust.

- Appropriate task delegation.

- Sound working/decision-making procedures.

- Regular planning and review processes.

- Opportunities for individual development.

- Sound inter-group relationships.

- Good leadership.

- The right people, with the right range of skills where diversity and difference are valued.

- Each member understands theirs and their team mate's roles.

- Clear objectives and agreed team goals.

- Results are measured and acknowledged.

- Individual effort is acknowledged.

- People are praised for being team players.

- Good communication and information exchange between all members and problems are not allowed to fester unresolved.

- Everyone is able to take advantage of collective and shared skills of members so that everyone to works together to achieve greater results than individuals working on the same objectives.

Teams are Made Up of Individuals

When each individual takes part in team and work activities they need to think not only about themselves but also their team mates and the group's overall goals. Remember, even if you're a manager or the business owner, you're still a member of the team; and as a member of the team your role is to:

- Communicate clearly, respecting other people's viewpoints.

- Think about team goals as well as personal goals.

- Focus on the team's purpose.

- Listen carefully and sensitively to others in the team.

- Develop a rapport with team mates that shows respect and trust.

- Participate and get involved in the team's processes.

- Set achievable goals for yourself and the team.

Teamwork Raises the Standard of Customer Service

Many organisations find that teams can better service the needs of customers than individuals can. Members of a well-functioning team support one another, provide back up and collaborate to improve the quality of the product or service they are passing on to their customers. So what can be done to promote effective teamwork?

- An objective and fair reward system should be established. Rewards can motivate staff, make them feel appreciated and increase their resilience.

- Regular training and coaching should be provided as standard practice and not just be on a need-to-know basis.

- Team support can be developed through regular meetings. A well-run meeting can help a team to feel purposeful and keep a sense of direction. The leader needs to involve all team members in active participation and use people's strengths to the advantage of the team.

- Identify resources required to undertake team tasks while meeting required customer service levels.

Create a Customer Intelligence Engine

Give your team what they need to deliver excellent customer service: turn your website and associated online data and turn it into a dynamic customer intelligence engine.

Take all of your customer touch points into account, and then connect the dots. In a business setting, a customer is a department or firm, rather than simply a collection of individuals. You need to pay attention to the inter-relationships among the multiple people, and develop a collective view about the group as a whole. And you need to pay attention to the complete life cycle of the relationship – from pre-sales to post sales, service and support, and ways to continue to engage and enhance the experience over time.

Remember content personalisation is an interactive process. You'll get better over time. Focus first on a few high value scenarios. Tailor the content to address these conversations. Track your results and learn from your customers' experiences. Then refine the content delivery for these initial scenarios, and develop new ones.

You'll quickly assemble a valuable collection of scenarios and enhance your understanding of what your customers need. You'll also be able to create new conversations that extend the scope and capabilities of your online presence.

Learn from your customers' responses. Through these conversational exchanges, you shape the interactive experiences for your customers.

> **Step 1 –** Identify your customer's needs. To implement effective customer service training with employees, you first need to know what your customers expect from your staff and what their needs generally are. This can be accomplished by giving each customer a comment card, setting up a ratings or feedback section on your company's website, and/or asking customers about their experience with your company on their last visit and past visits. You also may elect to hire a survey firm that conducts customer satisfaction surveys.

> **Step 2 –** Evaluate each employee's skills and skill level. Some employees will be natural salespersons and possess the skills to up-sell customers with little effort. Others will be better at problem solving or pre-emptive problem solving in which they are able to identify when a customer is unhappy or unsatisfied and address the situation before it becomes unmanageable. Study your employees and identify which have the best skill sets for a particular customer service need, such as establishing a rapport and up-selling. Conduct regular meetings allowing, each employee to showcase and explain how they carry out their particular skill set.

> **Step 3 –** Design and implement a training method. This can be done just as in the example of allowing employees to individually demonstrate their skill set and how they execute it effectively. You can also record via video or audio transcription a text of the employee's presentation or use it to compile a customer service manual. You can also have experienced employees or supervisors or managers shadow new employees, and train them on the job.

> **Step 4 –** Re-evaluate your employee's customer service relations on a consistent basis. Employee evaluations should be given at least twice a year to as many as once a quarter. You want to allow the employee to give feedback on their evaluation and by the same token, allow them input on how effective they believe the customer service training to be. You want to ensure each employee is complying with the company's customer service protocol. For instance, Walmart employees are required to greet any customer that comes within 20 feet of an employee within seven to 10 seconds.

Implement an External Strategy

The external strategy should focus on how your agency's service is designed, marketed, and delivered to target customers.

Take into account the costs of providing services and ways to minimise those costs while implementing quality control. Develop the service concept with the frontline worker at its centre. Determine the necessary financial, human, and technological resources, as well as how your agency structure and flow can enable frontline workers to deliver excellent customer service.

Use advertising/educational strategies to set appropriate customer expectations.

Provide a feedback loop to incorporate customer comments and complaints into the planning process. Customer complaints are an invaluable resource. Without them, organisations can't be successful. Complaints that people bring to your agency are one of the most efficient and least expensive ways to get information about people's expectations of your agency and its products and services. Studies have shown that customer comments and complaints are a more direct means of getting information than conducting research studies of customer expectations, conducting transaction studies, or reviewing customer expectations in similar industries.

Ensure that the complaint resolution strategy supports the customer-focused vision. Most research shows if customers believe their complaints are welcomed and responded to, they will more likely come back to your organisation for a future interaction.

Personalising Content Delivery

You have a lot of flexibility with the customer experience framework to control your customer intelligence engine. It's important to target the content you deliver over the web by developing and implementing personalisation rules. The collection of rule sets provides the capabilities to shape the customer experience.

Start with a few simple situations. Then steadily expand your pool of experience by scripting and deploying scenarios for action.

> EXAMPLE – AAMI Customer Charter 2013
>
> The AAMI Customer Charter, first introduced in 1996, encompasses AAMI's commitment to always provide its customers with the highest standards of customer service.
>
> AAMI has a customer base of over 3 million car insurance and home insurance policies, over 300,000 insurance claims in the year and millions of incoming telephone calls. The Charter has been recognised for its integrated delivery of business process development, top class customer service and the protection of consumer rights. The following are example sections from the AAMI Customer Charter:

Accessibility: We will be available 24 hours a day, seven days a week. Simply call us on 13 22 44.

Personal Information: We value the personal information you give us and will take all reasonable precautions to prevent unauthorised access to that information.

Car Claims Service Guarantees: The quality of workmanship and the materials authorised by AAMI in the repair of your car will be guaranteed for the life of the car. When we recommend our Valet Service for your car claim, for no extra cost, we will: pay for your taxi to home or work after you deliver your car to our assessment centre make all the necessary repair arrangements for you.

Home Claims Service Guarantees: When the home you permanently live in is damaged by an event covered under your Home Building Insurance Policy, and we agree it is unliveable, we will: arrange emergency accommodation for you and your family arrange funds as an advance against your settlement, if required provide up to three trauma counselling sessions for you and your family, if required. If your contents are stolen from your home, we will contact you during the course of the claim to keep you informed. The quality of workmanship and the materials used in any repair or rebuilding of your home or contents that we arrange and authorise will be guaranteed for the life of the property.

Dispute Resolution: AAMI endeavours to resolve all disputes quickly and fairly. To assist in this, we maintain a free and accessible internal dispute resolution process. To use this service, call us on 13 22 44. For further details, please download a copy of our brochure titled What to do if you don't agree with our decision.

Our Commitment: The AAMI Charter 2013 commences on 1 January 2013 and only applies to policies (including renewals) commencing on or before 31 December 2012, as the majority of the Charter promises are now embedded in our latest Product Disclosure Statements. This Charter does not cover Business, Compulsory Third Party or any Life insurance products sold by AAMI. We're committed to our customers and striving to meet and exceed our Customer Charter promises. We regularly review our performance and commit to adherence to the Customer Charter with a contribution to the Suncorp Group's Brighter Futures Community Giving program which we will report on. You can read about our Brighter Futures Community Giving program at www.suncorpgroupbrighterfutures.com.au

Why Teamwork is the Route to Great Customer Service

Teams that are well organised and effectively managed are characterised by high morale, high productivity, and high levels of customer service.

To create an excellent customer service team, investment of time and resources is needed – regular training and coaching should be provided as standard practice and not just be on a need-to-know basis.

A team with both the skills and the knowledge to deliver a great service to the customer relies on a solid understanding of your customers' needs and expectations as well as being able to meet and surpass those needs and expectations through an understanding of the customer experience. At the end of the day, as with all teamwork, consistency is the key.

END OF CHAPTER ACTIVITY – Implement Team Customer Service Standards

1. Write a script for how you would like the phone to be answered. You will then have a document which you can give your new staff on induction.

2. If you want to take this a step further use your smartphone and video somebody actually doing the action and start a private YouTube channel just for staff.

Conclusion

Throughout my whole career, whether that be in employment or working for myself, relationships have been the key to good business. Those relationships are built on a combination of both speaking and listening. A salesperson engaged in a face-to-face dialogue instinctively knows how to listen and respond. Online, customers should experience a comparable interaction, where you add intelligence to your web presence.

Publishing content on your website, telling your customers what you can do for them, persuading them about your business benefits, and helping them to make the right choices, are only the first steps.

If you have not already start tracking reactions (the power of a CRM is endless) then learn about your customers' needs, and dynamically adapt the information you deliver online to address their interests and concerns. Through the power of continuing conversations and ongoing information exchanges, you add insight to your company's website, and transform it into a customer intelligence engine.

By understanding what your customer's expect from their interactions with you will be a step ahead of your competitors.

If you would like to sign up to my monthly newsletter with tips and tricks, head to my website www.lisaharrison.com.au.

Lisa Harrison

Recommended Reading

"Customer Experience in the Age of Digital Banking" by Geoff Galat

"Building a Business Culture to Deliver the Best Customer Service" by Douglas Hannah

"How to Win Customers and Keep Them for Life" by Michael Leboeuf

thesocialcustomer.com

Queensland Government Business & Industry Portal

– a comprehensive business resource for start-ups, expansions, HR and more: http://www.business.qld.gov.au/industry/ict

GLOSSARY

Added Value: Added Value is the extra, over and above the basic product or service offer that an organisation makes to its customers. This added value represents extra benefits that can truly delight the customers and keep them loyal.

Code of practice: Many trade associations and professional bodies have a code of practice that guides members on how they should conduct their business.

Competitive advantage: Although a competitor is an organisation that offers products or services that are similar to those offered by your organisation. Your organisation may have the competitive advantage.

Competitor: Most organisations are not the only ones that provide particular products or services. Most customers can choose to use the products or services of another organisation rather than yours.

Complaint: When a customer feels strongly enough that his or her customer expectations have not been met, he or she may make a complaint.

Consistent service: Customer satisfaction is affected by customer expectations about the service they will receive. If the customer service they receive is different from what they expected, there is always a danger that customer satisfaction will be lower than expected.

Continuous improvement: Many organisations try to keep ahead of competitors by providing better customer service. If competitors also do this, organisations have to keep improving their customer service to stay ahead. So the process of continuous improvement helps organisations to make sure this happens as a matter of routine.

Contract: A contract is an agreement between two parties that can be enforced by law. A contract does not have to be in writing but it is more difficult to prove if it is not.

Costs and resources: Delivering customer service involves an organisation in spending money and using resources such as staff time, equipment and materials. It is important for you to understand what costs and resources are involved in delivering customer service in your organisation.

Customer: A customer is somebody who receives customer service from a service deliverer.

Customer expectations: Customer expectations are what people think should happen and how they think they should be treated when asking for or receiving customer service.

Customer experience: Customer experience is what a customer feels and remembers about the customer service that he or she has received.

Customer feedback: Customer feedback is information about customer perceptions of customer service collected by the organisation from customers or given to the organisation by customers.

Customer loyalty: Some customers tend to return to the same service deliverer and this is customer loyalty. Obviously customer loyalty can be built up if the customer experience of an organisation has been good.

Customer relationship: A customer relationship forms as the result of a number of individual customer service transactions.

Customer rights: Once somebody has been recognised as a customer by law, he or she has certain legal rights. These change as the law changes but customer rights are generally increasing.

Customer satisfaction: Customer satisfaction is the feeling that a customer gets when he or she is happy with the customer service that has been provided.

Customer service: Customer service is the sum total of what an organisation does to meet customer expectations and produce customer satisfaction.

Customer service procedures: Customer service procedures are the routines and detailed steps an organisation uses to deliver its customer service. Some organisations have formal procedures in writing and use those to train staff and to monitor service.

Customer service system: A customer service system involves a number of customer service procedures together with the people and resources needed to make it work.

Data protection legislation: Information about customers that is stored by a service provider must be kept confidential and must be dealt with in accordance with the requirements of data protection legislation.

Disability discrimination legislation: Service providers must comply with disability discrimination legislation and show that they offer customer service that does not discriminate against customers with disabilities.

Equal opportunities legislation and regulation: Equal opportunities legislation and regulation sets out to ensure that staff and customers are not discriminated against for reasons of ethnic origin or gender.

External customer: An external customer is a customer from outside the organisation providing a product or service.

Frontline staff: Frontline staff are people who have direct contact with customers either face-to-face or at a distance.

Health and safety legislation: Service providers have obligations to ensure that reasonable steps have been taken to ensure the health and safety of customers.

Internal customer: An internal customer is somebody from the same organisation as the service provider.

Legislation: Any organisation offering products or services must abide by laws that affect their businesses.

Mission statement: A mission statement is a brief statement of the main purpose or mission of the organisation.

Organisation: Customer service is generally delivered by a group of people working together.

Problem: A problem in customer service happens when the customer service does not meet customer expectations.

Products and services: Organisations involved in customer service offer a mixture of products and services. Customer satisfaction results from the overall effect of what is offered.

Regulation: Any organisation offering products or services must abide by regulations that affect their businesses.

Reliable customer service: For some organisations it is most important to provide service that people can depend on with confidence.

Risk assessment: all the risks that may exist and assessing them for seriousness and for the likelihood of them happening

Sector: Private Sector/Public Sector /Voluntary Sector and Non-profit making sectors – many people swap between public/private/voluntary job roles during their working lives and therefore to know the difference between these kinds of sectors is important.

Service deliverer: A service deliverer is the person in an organisation seen by the customer as giving the customer service

Service offer: A service offer defines the extent and limits of the customer service that an organisation is offering.

Service promise: It would be easy to say that this is another term for 'service offer' but the word 'promise' implies rather more active focus and commitment on the part of the organisation offering the service.

Service provider: A service provider is an organisation that provides customer service.

Support staff: People who work for a service deliverer and play a part in providing customer service without frequent direct contact with the customer.

Systems model of an organisation: A way of looking at an organisation that focuses on the processes that the organisation manages.

Terms and conditions: A contract generally places detailed obligations on each party and these are described in the terms and conditions.

www.ingramcontent.com/pod-product-compliance
Lightning Source LLC
Chambersburg PA
CBHW070931180526
45168CB00003B/1037